CLU

12 Puzzling Stories to Investigate

Peter Clarke

Illustrated by Martin Pitts

Edward Arnold

© Peter Clarke 1986

First published 1986 by
Edward Arnold (Publishers) Ltd
41 Bedford Square
London WC1B 3DQ

Edward Arnold (Australia) Pty Ltd
80 Waverley Road
Caulfield East
Victoria 3145
Australia

British Library Cataloguing in Publication Data

Clarke, Peter
    Clues: 12 puzzling stories to investigate.
    1. English language – Examination,
    questions, etc.
    I. Title
    428.2   PE1112

    ISBN 0–7131–7499–4

Photoset in Century Schoolbook
by Northern Phototypesetting Co., Bolton
Printed and bound in Great Britain
by Richard Clay (The Chaucer Press) Ltd.,
Bungay, Suffolk

To the Teacher

In writing the stories and assignments for *Clues*, I have tried to offer both a challenge to the individual pupil's reading and understanding, and the opportunity for small-group discussion and investigation.

The following lesson pattern is suggested with these in mind:

Reading the story (silent reading) approx. 10–15 mins.

First impressions (individual written response) approx. 5–10 mins. Pupils will merely indicate an understanding (or lack of understanding) of what they have just read. In some stories, their response need be no longer than a single line; in others it may extend to half a page – but no more.

Discuss your answers (in small groups) approx. 10 mins. Pupils will read out their answers to each other, and then discussion should be based on questions such as these: 'Is everyone agreed?' 'What led us to the answer?' 'Was it the same clue or a different one?' 'Are there any remaining clues that we have overlooked?'

Investigating together (investigating the text further) approx. 15 mins. Pupils will locate the stated number of clues; establish why they are relevant; discuss different theories and make inferences; work out reasoned answers.

Conclusions (teacher's questions) approx. 5–10 mins. Questions from the teacher will ensure that the story is clear to all pupils.

To the Pupil

I want you to imagine for a minute that you have in front of you a comprehension exercise. The passage that you have to read is about a girl called Julie, and the first question asks you how old she is. Luckily it's simply answered, for in the passage it is stated clearly 'Julie is 13 . . .'

Unfortunately information is not always given to you so clearly and simply: often you are just given clues. Instead of saying 'Julie is 13 . . .', the passage may say something like this: 'Julie hoped she would be picked for the 3rd year netball team . . .'

Or this: 'In three years' time, Julie, you can leave school and look for a job!'

Or this: 'Happy birthday, Julie! What does it feel like to be a teenager at last?'

It is important to realise, therefore, that information isn't always presented to you in a form that you can recognise straight away. It is not because writers are being deliberately awkward. They are merely relying on you being a sharp reader. The older you become, the more you will appreciate books of all kinds if you have learned to *infer* – that is – to spot clues and come to sensible conclusions.

These twelve stories will test how well you can infer, and offer you plenty of practice.

Have fun!

Contents

The New Arrivals

The doctor had called that morning.

'Cheer up! It's only measles, my dear,' she said to me. 'There's a lot of it about at the moment.' Then she turned to my Mum. 'Keep her in bed for a few days, and make sure she's nice and warm.'

After the doctor left, my Mum came up to my room again.

'I'll ring the school,' she said. 'I'll tell them that you'll have to miss the 1st year match tomorrow.'

Then she went over to the window. As she drew the curtains back a little, she stopped for a moment and looked out.

'I think the new people are moving in next door! But I mustn't stare. In fact, I must go shopping straight away, or we won't have any tea tonight. Are you alright, Sally?'

'Yes, Mum. Don't fuss. I'm fine,' I said. I didn't want to miss our new neighbours.

As soon as my Mum had gone downstairs, I moved my bed closer to the window. I wasn't going to miss a thing!

'So tell me all about them!' my Mum said when she got back. 'I know you'll have them all worked out!'

'Mum!' I said, protesting. Then I said, 'Well, there's a dad a bit like our Dad. About the same age, and the same height. He's going bald, though. Then there's a mum, a bit like you, but she's really fat. They have a boy and a girl. He's about thirteen years old, and she's about our Liza's age, nine or ten . . .' Liza is my younger sister.

I told my Mum all about them: their furniture; the clothes they wore; the colour of their hair; their pets; and lots of other things. I couldn't wait to be over the measles, so I could meet them.

I carried on watching for the next three days, but everything went quiet. The postman called every day with a parcel or a letter for our new neighbours. Our doctor came, too. I thought she was coming to see me, but she called at their house instead. It started to snow, and the next morning the windows were frozen on the inside! Everyone stayed indoors, and I was getting bored.

Then, that night, I was woken up suddenly by shouts and bangs. They came from next door. I switched on my light and looked at my watch. It was just past three o'clock in the morning! The noises were coming from upstairs. Then I heard someone rushing downstairs. It was the husband. He was suddenly running down the path, and getting into his car. He was trying to start it, but it wouldn't start. Then he ran back in, and I heard him talking loudly in the hall. Then all went quiet. Then there was more shouting. It was the wife's voice . . .

Five minutes later, an ambulance arrived. How exciting! I was a bit frightened, too. Had the husband killed his wife in a fit of passion?

I watched as the ambulance men came out of the house with a stretcher. The wife was on it, but I couldn't see her move. The ambulance drove off in a great hurry. Then all was quiet.

As I tried to get back to sleep, I promised myself I wouldn't say a word to anyone. I was sure I was the only one in our family to have heard a thing. It was *my* secret!

Three days later, I was up and about. It was dinner time, and an ambulance drew up outside again. The woman, our new neighbour, got out. She was thinner, but alive! She was carrying something and smiling. Her husband, and the two children came running out of the house, and there was lots of kissing. Everyone was looking at the parcel that the woman was carrying. It was pink and soft-looking.

'Of course! How silly of me!' shouted Sally. 'It's obvious what's happened . . . !'

First impressions

Is it obvious?

Finish off what Sally is saying. Just a sentence or two. Then say where you had got to in the story when you realised.

If you think you have missed the point, don't worry! Try reading the story again more carefully. Where do you think the woman has been?

Discuss your answers

Read out your answers to each other.
Have you reached the same conclusion?
Was it the same clue that led you to it?

Investigating together

Now look through the story for 10 clues which support your conclusion. Everyone must join in.

Conclusions

Report back to the whole group.

In a Pickle

The bus was coming at last. Mrs Taylor got on with her heavy
shopping bag. She showed her Senior Citizens' card to the
driver, and made her way to the back. The bus was very
crowded, but she was lucky. There was a seat near the back.
Two large men were in the seat in front of her. One of them had
a beard. She didn't like men with beards. The two men were
talking. She could hear almost every word they were saying.
She wasn't a nosy person, as she explained to the Police
Sergeant later. She just couldn't help overhearing what they
were saying.

'I'm afraid it's a last minute job,' the man without the beard was saying. 'We're shooting "The Mafia in London", and Marlon doesn't feel he can manage the rough-stuff any longer. You'll be doing that part for him. Tomorrow. We'll start the shooting early.'

'So I'm going to be thrown in the deep end!' laughed the bearded man.

Both men laughed, and Mrs Taylor shivered. Who were these men? She edged a bit closer.

'So you'll do it?' said the first man. 'You're a true professional! It pays well, of course. £200 for two minutes' work can't be bad.'

'Tell me more,' said the bearded man. 'Is it to be fists or guns?'

'Both,' replied the first man. 'Marlon Brando's the Mafia boss. He's moving in on the London scene. He's challenged by the Kray Brothers who run the East End of London. This is where you come in. There's a fist-fight, but then the guns come out. Bullets are flying everywhere, blood, screams, bodies everywhere . . . the full works!'

Poor Mrs Taylor nearly had a heart attack! Guns, fights, shooting, the Mafia! It was all too much after a hard day's shopping! She was very relieved when the two men got off at the next stop. But she was so excited and confused that she missed her own stop altogether.

When she finally reached her local Police Station, she was in a terrible state. The Sergeant had to sit her down and give her a cup of tea.

When she had calmed down a little, the Sergeant sat down with a pencil and paper.

'Right, Mrs Taylor,' he was saying, 'there were two men. One had a beard. He was a professional hit-man. He was going to be paid £200 to kill a Mafia boss. Where was this going to take place?'

'In a swimming pool, I think. "Up the deep end," I heard one of them say. I think he said that, but I'm so confused,' said Mrs Taylor, shaking her head.

'Does this Mafia boss have a name, Mrs Taylor?' asked the Sergeant.

'Yes, a name was mentioned. Marlon Somebody. Marlon Branston or something like it,' said Mrs Taylor, pleased that her memory hadn't let her down.

'I think you mean Marlon Brando,' laughed the Sergeant. 'What would you say to another cup of tea, Mrs Taylor? Then I'll explain what a pretty pickle you've got into!'

$$\boxed{?}$$

First impressions

What will the Sergeant say to Mrs Taylor? Keep it short and to the point. No more than half a page.

If you think you may have missed the point, don't worry! Try reading the story again more carefully. As you read, ask yourself who the men on the bus were.

Discuss your answers

Read out your answers to each other.
Have you all reached the same conclusion? How?

Investigating together

Why do you think Mrs Taylor got it so wrong?
You should be able to find about 5 different reasons if you look carefully enough. Try to list the clues separately. Everyone must join in.

Conclusions

Report back to the whole group.

Gary's Note

It was Julie who found the note first. She had woken early and run into Gary's room. As soon as she had jumped on his bed, she realised that something was wrong. Instead of Gary, there were pillows under the bed clothes. When she switched the lamp on, she noticed that his teddy-bear was missing, and a note . . .

It read:

> I hav run away. i am fed up of being bossed. do not tri to find me cos you will never do it. i am never comming back you see
>
> luv gary
>
> ps i never brok our kevins train set, he did it hisself

'The daft little beggar!' muttered Dad, as Julie woke him with the news. 'What does he want to do a daft thing like that for?'

'You were too hard on him yesterday. I said so, didn't I?' said Mum, turning over in bed. 'What in heaven's name are you going to do?'

'Dad! Dad! It's been snowing in the night!' shouted Steve, the youngest, as he burst into the room. 'It's stopped now, but it's right deep! Will you take us sledging?'

'That's all we need!' said Dad, as he jumped out of bed. 'He'll freeze to death unless we get a move on. A perfect end to Christmas!'

'What will you do?' asked his wife, who was now wide awake and sitting up in bed.

'Once I'm dressed, I'll run down to the phone box. I'm going to ring the Police. While I'm gone, the rest of you get dressed. Get the kettle on, and get some breakfast on the table.'

Half an hour later, as the sun appeared, Sergeant Parsons arrived with his Alsatian dog, Oscar. First, he took down a description of Gary. Next, he wanted to know what Gary was wearing, and what he had taken with him.

'He's taken his teddy-bear with him!' shouted Julie straight away. She wanted to be helpful.

'Very good,' said the Sergeant, writing this down in his notebook. 'Is there anything else? Has he taken any money or food? We will need to have a very careful look,' he said.

After a few minutes, Sergeant Parsons had all the answers he wanted. He brought out his walkie-talkie, and called his station.

'Alpha 1 to Base. I am at Birch Cottages in Longton Village. I'm following up a young lad, Gary Morton, aged eight years, who has run off. He is wearing a pair of jeans, a brown duffel coat, and new pair of red wellingtons. He's taken his teddy-bear and a Mars bar, but nothing else. He has no money, nor a bag. I've got an old shirt of his, so I'll have a quick look round with Oscar, and report back in half an hour. I don't think the lad will be far away. No one's about yet, so it shouldn't be so difficult. Over!'

By half past eight, Gary was found in an old barn above the village. He was very cold, but a little disappointed.

'How did you find me so quick?' he asked.

'Well, it wasn't so hard,' said the Sergeant smiling. 'I thought you wouldn't be so far away . . .'

'Why?' Gary asked.

'Well, there were three main things, and I'll tell you as we walk home together. But first I must call the station . . .

?

First impressions

Write down what you think Sergeant Parsons will say to Gary as they walk home together. How will he explain to Gary how he has found him so quickly?

If you think you may have missed the point, try reading the story more carefully a second time. Try to imagine what Sergeant Parsons is thinking and planning.

Discuss your answers

Read out your answers to each other.
Are they similar?
Have you all come up with the same reason, or different ones?

Investigating together

Now look through the story again, and see if you can come up with 4 separate clues.

Additional questions

1. What information did Sergeant Parson want when he first called? Why would this information help him?
2. Why didn't the Sergeant think Gary would be far away?
3. Was the father right to be worried? Why?
4. Why do you think Gary ran away (several reasons)?
5. How many children are there in the family? How old do you think they might be? How can you tell?
6. Why did the Sergeant want a piece of Gary's clothing?

Conclusions

Report back to the whole group.

Sam's Slip

The warning bell had rung. A voice came over the loud-speaker. It was telling shoppers to hurry. The store was about to close. A quarter of an hour later, the staff were saying goodnight to each other. The faint sounds of their voices could be heard as they left the building. Johnson's, 'the store with a branch in every city', was in the middle of its January Sale. Many thousands of pounds had been taken that day. It was now safely stored in a large steel safe on the first floor. It was the end of another day . . . for some.

For others, the day was only just beginning. Security officers were already patrolling the store, checking that everyone had left. The cleaners would be starting their work in half an hour. And in a small, locked store-room on the first floor, Sam Fisher ('Slippery Sam' to the Police and prison warders) was waiting to start *his* day's work. He was planning on 'cleaning up' in a rather different way.

As he waited, Sam could hear a security man checking and locking every door. At last he reached the small store-room. The handle went down . . . and up again. Seconds later, Sam heard the next door being locked. Finally, he heard the man shout, 'All clear on the first floor, Jo!'

This was the signal for Sam to get his keys out. He knew he had half an hour before the cleaners arrived. He put on his silk gloves, and picked up his tool bag.

Quickly but quietly he unlocked the store-room with his master-key. He turned left down the corridor. At the bottom of the corridor, he stopped. No one was coming. He turned right. The second door on the right was the one he wanted. A quick snip with his wire-cutters shut off the burglar alarm. His keys opened the door. Inside the main office, there was a hidden camera on the wall. Sam adjusted this so that it now pointed at a smaller safe on another wall.

'This is going to be a doddle!' he thought to himself.

Five minutes later, as the last lever of the lock clicked, the safe was open. Sam's eyes lit up as he cast them over the thick bundles of notes. It took him only a few minutes to stack the bundles into his bag. Now it was finished, and he looked at his watch. Everything was going to plan, and he still had ten minutes to spare. He had time to cool down and relax. He took off his hat, scarf and gloves and put them in his bag. Then he took a small can of beer from his pocket.

Sam had nearly finished his beer, when he heard the faint sound of voices at the end of the corridor. He quickly got his things together. With his left hand on the large, brass door-knob, he eased the latch shut. With his right hand, he turned the key and locked the door.

His escape route was well planned: he slipped out through a small window, crossed the roof, and was down the fire escape in no time. There were no hitches.

As he reached his car, which he had parked in a side street, he remembered the can of beer in his pocket. After a single swallow, Sam wiped his lips with the back of his bare hand. He then burped loudly and tossed the empty can over a wall. It had gone well, and he felt pleased with himself.

At 10.30 the next morning, as Sam Fisher was still in bed, he was woken by a loud knocking on his front door. Two police officers took him to the local police station where he was charged with stealing £20,000 from Johnson's Store.

Only later, when he appeared in court at his trial, did he learn how he had 'slipped up'.

?

First impressions

'In court, the police witness said . . .'

Finish this off, saying what evidence the police had against Slippery Sam. No more than five lines.

If you're not sure, don't worry. Read the story again more slowly. As you read, ask yourself:
'Has he made his mistake yet . . . ?'

Discuss your answers

Sam made just one mistake. Did you manage to spot it?

Investigating together

Sam made one mistake, but there are 2 clues to this mistake. Did you find them both? If not, go back to the story and investigate.

Additional questions

1. Sam had planned this burglary carefully. At least 5 clues tell you this. Can you find them?
2. Has Sam Fisher been in trouble with the law before? How can you tell? (2 clues)
3. Was Johnson's a good target to rob? Why?
4. What time of year was it? How do you know?
5. Why do you think Sam Fisher is called 'Slippery Sam'?

Conclusions

Report back to the whole group.

Don't Shoot!

Patch had been our dog for nearly three years. He was really my dog. He had been the last of the litter belonging to my friend Jenny Watson's dog. He was going to be 'put down' because no one wanted him. I had nagged my Mum and Dad for days. At last they had given in.

'Alright, Sarah,' my Mum had said at last. 'As long as *you* feed him and take him for walks every day. Proper walks through the fields and up on the moors. And not just on fine days, in *all* weathers. It will be a responsibility.'

No one would say he was beautiful, but he was lovable. He was a mongrel. Jenny's dog was a black and white Border Collie bitch, a proper working sheepdog on a local farm. Patch's father must have been a terrier. You could tell by the coarser hair and the long whiskers. Jenny's father hadn't been very pleased. He had kept his bitch on a chain in the farmyard. He had been waiting to mate her with a pure-bred sheepdog.

I had a name for him straight away. He had a big, black mark over his left eye, so I called him Patch. At first, Mum went mad because he chewed the armchair cushions. In the summer he moulted, leaving his hairs all over the carpet, but she got used to him. She even took him for walks some days.

He was a very obedient dog. Whenever I called, he came running. When I took him off his lead, he always stayed close to me . . . until last Sunday when he ran off.

We looked everywhere: Jenny's farm; the estate where most stray dogs ended up; the park by the Civic Hall. I even went as far as the school. We rang everyone we knew, and asked them to look out for him. It was winter and very cold outside. I worried about him as I lay in bed that night, listening to the wind.

When I woke up early the next morning, I prayed he would

be waiting for me on the doorstep. He wasn't.

I was miserable at school all day.

'What's this? Monday morning blues?' asked Mrs Hoyle, my form teacher. I started to tell her about Patch, but I burst into tears. She said she would let me ring home at dinner time, using the school phone.

Dinner time came, but Patch still hadn't come home.

'Don't worry!' Mrs Hoyle told me. 'He's probably having a wonderful time chasing other dogs. He'll be off for a few days, and come back when he's had enough.'

I wanted to believe her, but I was afraid that he had been knocked down by a car or a lorry.

At tea-time on Wednesday, there was a loud knock on the door. I rushed to open it. It was Mr Mitchell, a local farmer. He was looking serious.

'Is your dog around, is he?' he asked.

'No,' I said.

'Know where he is, do you?' he asked, giving nothing away.

'He's run off,' I said. 'We've looked everywhere for him.'

'He's been with my sheep, worrying them. Yesterday early morning, and again today, just one hour since. I'll have to speak to your Dad about it. You see it's my sheep that I'm worried about.'

I called my Dad and went inside.

Half an hour later, Mr Mitchell left.

'It looks bad,' my Dad said, as he came into the kitchen. 'Both Mr Mitchell and Mr Lee reckoned they saw Patch. There were three dogs running together. His sheep are early in lamb and he . . . well . . .' Dad was shaking his head.

'He wants Patch shot, doesn't he?' I cried.

'Yes, that's about it. And he'll want me to pay if he loses any lambs as a result.'

'Patch wouldn't chase sheep! I know he wouldn't! I've taken him all through Mr Mitchell's fields lots of times, and he's never bothered them!'

'Dogs can be very different when they are together, Sarah,' my Dad explained. 'I think we will have to prepare for the worst. I'm sorry.'

23

The next day we were sitting gloomily having tea, when my Dad said, 'I suppose I could try to find out if he's been picked up by the local dog-handler and been taken to a dogs' home.'

When my Dad started phoning, I went into the kitchen. I couldn't bear to listen. My Dad's voice was very faint, but I could still hear a part of what he was saying. He was describing Patch. Then I heard him say, 'Yes, yes, yes.' Then there was a long wait when no one spoke. Then my Dad said, 'Oh fine, thank you very much.'

As my Dad came through into the kitchen, he was smiling.

'They think they've got him. They've got a dog that fits his description. The ink on his name-tag has run, but it's a yellow tag. Let's get going!'

When I saw Patch, I cried and hugged him. It was Patch alright. No doubt! We had to pay £6 to get him out – £2 for every night he had spent there. Poor Patch! He looked very dirty and hungry.

When I got him home, I washed him all over, gave him a good meal, and then took him for a nice walk – on a lead!

The next day, soon after tea, there was another knock on the door. Patch barked and growled. Mr Mitchell and Mr Lee stood on the doorstep. Mr Mitchell had a gun under his arm.

'Your dog's back then, Sarah,' he said.

'Yes,' I said after a little pause. It was no use lying.

'We'll just be having a word with your father. Be a good girl and fetch him.'

I fetched my Dad, and went back inside. My Dad was holding Patch by the collar. He was shivering.

I went into the front room, and the tears came flooding through my eyes. It was so unfair. I couldn't bear to think of Patch being shot.

After a short while, the tears passed off and I got to my feet. I crossed over to the door and listened. They were still there at the door, talking. Patch was letting out little whimpers. I leant my head against the glass of the hall door. My eyes came to rest on a piece of paper on the hall table. It was the receipt from the dog's home. 'One black and white mongrel – £6. Paid with thanks. J. Jones (Warden).'

Suddenly I was through the door and into the hall.

'Wait!' I shouted. 'You can't shoot Patch! He couldn't have chased your sheep . . .'

?

First impressions

Why not? What reason can she give?
Finish off the story. Write down what Sarah says to Mr Mitchell and Mr Lee, and (briefly) what happens after that. No more than half a page.

If you can't think of the reason, you will have missed the point. Don't worry, try reading the story again more carefully. Keep asking yourself where Patch has got to . . .

Discuss your answers

Read out your answers to each other.
Had Patch chased sheep?
What is the evidence?

Investigating together

It often helps in puzzling situations like this to set out the relevant information in another, clearer form.

Draw a plan like the one below, and fill in the main events of the story, day by day. The first entry is done for you.

SUNDAY	Patch runs off
MONDAY	
TUESDAY	
WEDNESDAY	
THURSDAY	
FRIDAY	
SATURDAY	

Remember the dog-handler!

Next work out together what kind of place Sarah and her family lived in. There are 7 clues that will help you to build up quite a detailed picture – if you're careful.

Additional questions

1. How could Mr Mitchell have thought it was Patch who had been worrying his sheep?
2. Why didn't the Dogs' Home ring up Sarah's Dad?
3. Why do you think Mr Lee came round on the Friday?
4. How did Mr Mitchell know that Patch had come back?

Conclusions

Report back to the whole group.

A Slip of the Tongue

The bell for morning break rang. Three short rings and then a fourth, longer ring. Mr Carson, the teacher, got up from his desk and spoke to the class.

'Right! Books and pens away now! John, Karen and Nicky, I want you to collect in the exercise books. There are still a number of calculators and protractors that need to be brought back . . .'

A minute later, the class was dismissed.

Karen tidied up her things slowly. She was in no rush to leave. She had brought something in to show Mr Carson. It was a gold locket and chain that her great-aunt had left her. Mr Carson knew all about the marks stamped onto real gold objects, she had discovered. He had suggested that she might bring it to school one day if her parents agreed. She had brought it in a small leather box, lined with red velvet on the inside. As she opened up the box, however, her heart sank. The box was empty!

'What do you want me for?' asked Louise, as she was brought into the classroom alone five minutes later.

'Sit down, Louise,' said Mr Carson in a friendly manner. 'A very expensive locket and chain has disappeared. I'm wondering if you have seen it?'

Louise thought about this, but didn't answer at first.

'Do you know anything about it?' carried on Mr Carson.

'Of course I don't. I haven't seen any stupid locket and chain. That's the truth!'

'So you haven't seen it? Not at all, Louise?' added Mr Carson.

'I said "no", didn't I? Has Karen been saying that I took it? If so, she's a liar!'

'Alright! Alright!' said Mr Carson. 'As it happens, she hasn't accused anyone.'

'Well, why are *you* accusing me?' asked Louise.

'I am not accusing you, Louise. I am just asking you a few questions, that's all. I need to find this locket and chain. You were sitting next to Karen, and you never left your seat, so . . .'

'So?' interrupted Louise. 'There were loads of other people who knew she had it. Angela, Rachel, Susan. She was showing us all before the lesson.'

Mr Carson paused for a moment.

'Have you any idea how much a pure silver locket and chain is worth these days?' he asked.

'Gold!' said Louise, correcting him.

'Well, how much?' asked Mr Carson. 'Have a guess.'

'About £20,' suggested Louise, after thinking for a moment.

'I would say it would be more like £120, Louise. And I think it is about time you started telling me the truth, don't you?'

Louise went very quiet for a few moments.

'What would you say if I asked you to let me look through your bag?' Mr Carson asked, breaking the silence.

'Go ahead! Take a look. You won't find anything. I'm not that stupid!' she snapped.

'Louise, let's stop playing games, shall we? I know you've taken it. You see you've slipped up in several of the things that you've just told me . . .'

First impressions

Explain how Mr Carson knows that Louise has stolen the locket and chain. Finish off what he is saying. No more than five lines.

If you're not sure, you've probably missed the clues in the text. Don't worry, go back to the story and read it more carefully this time. Keep thinking how Mr Carson knows. There is more than one possible answer.

Discuss your answers

Read out your answers to each other.
Have you all come up with the same reason(s)?
Have you all answered the question about *stealing*?
There could be as many as 5 clues if you list them separately.

Or have you answered the different question: 'How did Mr Carson know that Louise had been *lying*?'

Investigating together

Louise made a number of slips while talking to Mr Carson. Have you found all of them? There are 5 clues in what was said. And are there any clues in Louise's attitude and behaviour? Discuss all these points amongst yourselves.

Additional questions

1. What subject do you think Mr Carson taught?
2. When could the locket and chain have been stolen?

3. 'You were sitting next to Karen, and you never left your seat, so . . .' What is Mr Carson trying to say?

Conclusions

Report back to the whole group.

There's Always a Catch...

Arthur Morris was very good at his job. Even the Police agreed he was about the best explosives man in the business. No one knew more about gelignite than Arthur. He was just short of luck. All his working life he was dogged by bad luck (or so he always said).

He never gave the law any trouble. Never any fighting or rough-stuff. They never had to drag the truth out of him. Once he was caught, he told them everything. Well, nearly everything.

'I had planned this little job months ago,' he told them. 'Nice little bank near the railway station. Just right for me, I think you'll agree. Nice and easy to get in. Alarm system, no problem. Near the station for a quick getaway. First class train ticket to London, and Bob's your uncle!'

'I'd planned it for April 10th. Yes, I know it's now May 15th, but things went wrong. I'm coming to that! Anyway, I'd come up from London on April 9th. Last minute check, you know. I got there about dinner time, and blow me! There was a van outside the bank. "Ace Alarms" it said, "The Best in the Business." There were a couple of young fellas on ladders outside. Fixing some wires to the wall, they were.

'Well that was a surprise I could have done without! Now I had to do some homework. A few phone calls, a lot of reading and thinking. All this took time. I never hurry, you know that. Not my style. Too many mistakes are made when people start tearing around.

'All this takes me over a month. But I was ready then. May 15th. That was the new date I set. It was a Thursday, you see. Wages day Friday? I'm not so daft as you think. Anyway I came up from London on the 14th. Stayed in a nice little place I know. No questions asked, you understand. Kept watch on the bank all day. "Keeping it under surveillance" I think you coppers call it, don't you?

'Well everything was just fine. At 6 o'clock I got into the bank at the back. No, don't ask me how, because I won't tell you *all* my little secrets. A trick of the trade, you might say. A snip here, and a snip there, and those smart new burglar alarms wouldn't sing any more. Pity for those nice young lads who put them in. I reckon they won't be asked back!

'Anyway, I settled down by the safe. No problems. Nice little bang and no mess. All the notes in nice, neat bundles all ready for me. It was all over in a few minutes. "Arthur," I says to myself, "it hardly seems right. It's like stealing from a baby!"

'I looked at my train timetable again – just to check. The quarter-past-seven train would be waiting for me, I thought. I had my ticket all ready in my pocket. I'm a professional, see!

'I arrived with my suitcase at five minutes past seven. And you know what? There was no London train there!

' "You've missed it," they said. "It went five minutes ago. The next one isn't until tomorrow morning."

' "Look here!" I said, "that's no damn good to me. It's the 7.15 tonight that I'm interested in, and it's printed here in black and white!"

INTER CITY TRAIN SERVICES					*until 14th May* Weekdays only						
Manchester Piccadilly	10.15	11.53	13.15	14.15	15.15	15.35	16.13	16.42	17.12	18.15	19.15
Stockport	10.23	12.03	13.23	14.23	15.23	15.43	16.21	—	17.20	18.23	19.24
Wilmslow	—	—	13.31	—	15.31	—	—	16.57	—	18.31	—
Macclesfield	10.37	12.17	—	14.37	—	15.57	16.35	—	17.35	—	19.38
Stoke-on-Trent	10.57	12.37	—	14.57	—	16.17	16.55	—	17.55	—	19.58
Milton Keynes	—	—	—	—	17.18	—	—	—	—	—	—
Watford Junction	—	—	—	—	17.46	17.57	18.30	18.54	19.35	20.42	21.33
London Euston	12.58	14.44	16.08	17.00	18.08	18.20	18.54	19.14	19.57	21.04	21.55

'I showed it to them, but do you know what? They just laughed. Told me there was a train leaving for Timbuctoo in a few minutes. Cheeky devils!

'Well, I had a cup of tea, and I thinks things out.

'Arthur, old son, you can't go walking through town with a six figure sum in your suitcase. You'd best leave it at the "Left Luggage Office" before it's too late.

'So that's just what I did. Only the fellow there was too damned clumsy.

'"Steady on!" I told him. "There's something valuable in there! The catch isn't . . ."'

'He snatched the case all the same. Real rough. I warned him, but like I said, he snatched it from me.

'Dear, oh dear! It hurts just to think about it. I just closed my eyes and waited for you boys . . .'

?

First impressions

Explain to Arthur why he'd missed his train. No more than two sentences.

If you're not sure, read the story again with this at the front of your mind. *Check all his planning extra-carefully.*

Discuss your answers

Read out your answers to each other.
Did you all get the same reason?
Discuss any doubts you may have.

Investigating together

What had gone wrong with Arthur's plans? He might have got away with it, if only . . .

Try to find 4 'if only' reasons for his failing.

Additional questions

1. Where was the bank? In which city?
2. Was this Arthur's first job? How can you tell?
3. Why did he have to change the date of the robbery?
4. How do we know Arthur has stolen a lot of money?

Conclusions

Report back to the whole group.

The Chase

Some kids live miles from their school. I'm lucky, I suppose. My house is in Station Road, and it's only about a quarter of a mile away. It's quickest if I go along the Bolton Road. I do this most days, stopping at the sweet shop on the way.

Tonight I was with Craig and his sister, Linda. Craig said there were loads of conkers on Belfield Crescent. This is a long, curved road that leaves the Bolton Road just next to the school, and comes out lower down by the station. It has houses on the left hand side only. On the other side are trees and a great high fence stopping people from getting onto the railway.

We had plenty of conkers already. We'd got them at dinner time from the park. They were bulging out of our pockets.

Craig and I were walking ahead. Linda had stopped to do up her shoe lace. Then, the next thing, I felt this hard thing land on the back of my head. I grabbed for one of my conkers and threw it back. So did Craig. Soon we were charging all over the place, throwing our conkers at each other.

I don't know who threw the one that hit the window. There was a terrible crash of broken glass, and we all stopped dead. It was about the third house along. The front window.

A second later, a man came out, quick as a flash. Then a big lad of about sixteen, then another lad, even bigger!

We didn't hang around! We heard the man's shouts. Then we set off as if a pack of hounds was after us. I don't know about the others, but I didn't look back. I just ran as fast as my legs would carry me. My heart was pounding. It was fit to explode! There was a dreadful pain in my side, too.

After a bit, we slowed down. Somehow I knew we weren't being chased any more. I wondered if one of them had rung the Police.

Craig urged me on.

'Don't hang around, Robbo!' he gasped. 'They've got a car. I

saw them get in it!'

'Oh, Lord. I'm ready to drop,' I said. 'How much further to the main road?'

I hadn't realised, until now, how long Belfield Crescent was. My school bag was weighing a ton. It was full of homework books and my football kit.

'Not far now!' shouted Linda.

We'd shaken them off, but all the same I was looking behind me as I ran. 'We've nearly made it,' I was telling myself.

Suddenly I felt a terrible bump. All the wind was knocked out of me for a few seconds. At first, I thought I'd bumped into a tree or a brick wall. It felt that hard. Then I tried to move, and I realised I was being held.

'Let me go!' I gasped at last.

'You're not going anywhere, son. Not until I learn which of you charlies is going to pay for my broken window.'

First impressions

Write the story from the man's point of view. He is sitting in his front room having a cup of tea, when there is a terrible crash . . .
Keep it short – no more than half a page.

If you are not very sure about what has happened, read the story again more carefully. Keep asking yourself what the man did after his window was broken. Can you picture it clearly enough?

Discuss your answers

If your answers are short enough, read them out to each other. If not, try to establish:

> who had caught the three children;
> how they'd managed it;
> how the schoolchildren had been outsmarted;
> the names of the three children.

Investigating together

It often helps when a picture isn't clear, to set out the information you have been given in a clearer, more manageable form. So, prepare a map of the locality to go with the story. Everyone must help.

The map should show:

> the school
> Belfield Crescent
> Bolton Road
> the man's house
> the railway
> the station
> Station Road
> where the children were caught
> the sweet shop

You are not *told* exactly where all these roads and buildings are. There are just small hints – you must *infer*. Anyway, do your best, and discuss everything as you go along.

Conclusions

Report back to the whole group.

The Bus-pass

'For the last time, Michael, get up! You've got to go to town, and be back by the time your Gran arrives!' shouted my Mum up the stairs.

'Alright! Alright! I'm coming!' I called back sleepily, snatching a final few seconds in bed.

'Your Dad will be up with a bowl of cold water if you're not down in *one* minute!'

I leapt out of bed. This wasn't just a threat. My Dad would really do it!

'The bus goes in five minutes!' my mother repeated. 'Now are you clear what I want you to do?'

'Yes, Mum!' I said.

'Well, just go over it for me. I want to know for sure.'

'Okay,' I said, 'but I'm not stupid, you know! You want me to get off at the stop before the Bus Station. I'll take your prescription – please note one neatly folded prescription safely tucked in top pocket – to the chemist in the High Street. I'll then take myself to the Town Hall Offices and get a new bus-pass.'

'Make sure you cross on the zebra crossing in front of the Town Hall. The main entrance is right opposite, and the lifts are just inside. Remember it's the 6th floor. Have you got your form?' my Mum asked.

'Yes, Mum!' I said, but I remembered that I needed a passport photo. I could have that done in the chemist's.

'Your bus fare? Oh, dear! Where's my purse? Here's £2.20 for my pills. They're the usual ones. And 50p for the bus. Now get a move on!'

At the chemist's I handed in my Mum's prescription, and I was told it would be ready in a few minutes. I was just walking over to the Quick-Snap booth, when I met Gary. We both had our photographs taken. Mine looked awful because Gary kept making me laugh. He was on his way to the United v City game, so I walked with him down to the Bus Station. When I met Steve, Terry and the rest of them, I wished I was going, too. They tried to persuade me as we went down the escalators to the Bus Station under the Town Hall. I waited with them until the Manchester bus arrived. Then I went to my stop. Five minutes later, as my bus arrived, I remembered the bus-pass.

At the bottom of the escalators, I noticed a lit-up sign which said, "Lifts to Town Hall Offices". I was in luck! There was a lift already there, waiting to go up. Several other people got on with me. I pressed the button for the 6th floor. The others pressed for different floors. The lift doors closed, and the lift zoomed up one floor, leaving my stomach behind. People were getting out, and others getting in. The lift was off again. It stopped a second time, then a third and a fourth time. A little bell rang as the lift reached a new floor. I was counting to six. The lift stopped a fifth time. Just one more floor to go, I thought.

There were no signs that I could see, as I stepped out of the lift. I was hoping for a nice big sign saying "Bus-passes", but there were just long corridors with hundreds of small offices with their doors closed. People moved busily from one office to another. No one seemed to notice me.

At last someone did stop, and I asked where to go. He was an elderly man with silver-grey hair.

'Wrong floor!' he boomed. 'Ask at Reception! It'll be quickest in the long run, young man. *I* still get lost if I set foot outside my little cage, and I've worked here more years than I care to remember! Come to think of it,' he added, pausing for a moment and looking at his watch, 'almost everyone is going off for their lunch.'

'I got my bus-pass alright,' said Julie, as we travelled back on the bus together, 'but I've got brains . . .'

'My Mum will go mad,' I said, ignoring Julie. 'I'm late for dinner. Gran's probably arrived, and I wasn't there to help her up the steps. I've not got my bus-pass! And, oh Lord, there's something else, too . . .!'

First impressions

What else had Michael forgotten? Finish off his sentence, and then say why he had made the mistake. Keep it short. None of you should need to read the story again for this answer.

Discuss your answers

Read out your answers to each other. Did you manage to find this easy clue?
Discuss any differences of opinion or any doubts you may have.

Investigating together

Using the evidence given in the story, put together a simple, side-on view drawing of the Town Hall Building, with its offices and Bus Station. Label these, and the different floors that the lift went to.

Now work out why Michael failed to get his bus-pass, and how he had managed to get to the wrong floor. Which floor had he ended up on?

Conclusions

Report back to the whole group.

The Dream Holiday

Nowhere had the letter given a reason. After several minutes
staring at it, Henry Ramsbottom rose and crossed to the
sideboard. The papers that the TV company had sent him
were there somewhere. He found them in the top drawer.
'Rules for playing *Your Turn Now*,' it said at the top of the
printed sheet. They'd sent him two copies with the entry form.
One he had signed and sent back. The other he had kept. There
were hundreds of small clauses to read, so he settled down at
the table with his glasses on.

As he read down the list, he muttered out loud.

'I'm not under 18 or over 65. I'm fit and healthy, no heart
complaints. I'll have to pass a screen test. Well, I did that.
Mustn't drink before the show. Must look smart on the show!
They must think they're dealing with a bunch of idiots!' he
commented bitterly. 'Must turn up at least an hour before the
show . . .'

The list seemed endless, but he was nearing the end.

He mustn't have taken part in any other TV quiz game; he
mustn't be related to, or know anyone who worked for the TV
company. Finally, there was a bit about claiming expenses.

'No, no, not that I know of, certainly not,' Henry was
muttering as he came to each new clause.

'Well, it beats me,' he said finally, shaking his head. 'There
must be some mistake.'

They'd persuaded him to apply, his friends at the pub. They
had all been watching the programme in the saloon bar. They
were asking for new people to take part in the next series.
Henry had sent for the forms, and filled them in.

Then a letter had arrived a fortnight later. They wanted
him for a screen test. They would pay his travel expenses, they
said. Henry hadn't been too keen, but his family pushed him.

'Go on with you!' his wife had said. 'It'll be a laugh! Have a go, man!'

So he had gone.

On his return, he declared the screen test 'a load of rubbish'. But when another letter arrived a month later, with a London postmark, he had opened it with great excitement. They wanted him on the programme after all!

Henry himself was not particularly bothered about his appearance, or about winning.

'As long as I do my best, I won't shame anyone,' he declared. But his wife had other ideas.

'You'll have a new suit, and no arguing!' she insisted. 'You may not be bothered, but I am. You'll get into training right away!'

Training?

Henry was to start jogging, and he was to have general knowledge questions fired at him at breakfast, tea and supper.

'What does EEC stand for?'

'What country uses rupees for money?'

'What is the capital of the Hawaian Islands?'

Every member of Henry's family had a store of questions ready at mealtimes. His wife became his manager.

'I won't have you fail. Not like last time,' his wife said.

And it paid off!

In Round 1, Henry scored top marks. He agreed to come back again the next week.

His second appearance was nearly as successful. He slipped up on a couple of questions – how to spell 'ukelele', and Mrs Thatcher's husband's first name. But he'd still won.

Back in his home village in Lancashire, Henry was a hero. He was getting fan-mail, too. From old friends, and even from members of his family that he'd never met! A distant cousin, on his father's side, had written a 10-page letter. It turned out, by an amazing coincidence, that he was one of the cameramen on the programme.

Henry had already won a TV, a video-recorder and a washing-machine. His third appearance would be his last. If he won again, he would win prizes worth much more. He would have a choice between a small electric car, a small yacht and a 4-berth caravan. But if he then went to 'Double or Quits' at the end, there would be a choice between a family holiday or an expensive saloon car. If he lost, he'd lose all his recent winnings. He daren't think about it.

As the final approached, Henry became more nervous. He complained of pains in his chest, and the doctor gave him some pills and told him to take it easy on the jogging. It was a touch of Angina, whatever that was. He'd cut his jogging down to once a day, and the pain had gone.

The send-off at the railway station on the morning of the big day was more like a royal send-off. Family, friends, the Mayor, the town's brass band, local TV, press photographers. He was made to pose for several different pictures. One shaking hands with the Mayor; another being kissed by the recently crowned Miss Rochdale; and yet another, for one of the more popular Fleet Street papers, wearing a flat cap and drinking a pint of northern bitter.

And Henry didn't let them down on the programme. As all his supporters watched on TV, the answers still came out right.

The first question had nearly stumped him:

'What was the name of the dog which was the first space traveller?'

His mind went a blank. Then it came.

'Laika!'

'Correct!'

He was back on top form. The answers continued to come.

'Now, Henry. This question to win a 4-berth caravan, a small yacht or the latest electric motor car: Who was killed when her long scarf was caught in . . .?'

'Isadora Duncan!'

'Correct!'

Henry was sweating. His family and friends back in Lancashire were jumping up and down.

'Go for it!' his wife was screaming. 'Go for the jackpot, Henry!'

'Now, Henry,' the presenter was saying. 'This is a big moment, eh? They'll be rooting for you back home, I daresay.'

'I'll say!'

'Henry, you have a simple choice. It's "Double or Quits" time. I want you to think about this choice very carefully . . .'

'I'll go on,' Henry said without hesitation.

There were cheers and whistles from the studio audience. Everyone liked a sport.

'Now, Henry. Take your time on this one. It's a very important answer you'll be giving me. Right? What is the capital city of the Hawaian Islands?'

'Honolulu!' snapped Henry.

'Correct!'

Henry wiped his brow. The audience went wild. His family back home danced up and down and kissed each other. Their Dad had done it!

But it wasn't all over yet. The presenter called for quiet.

'Henry, many congratulations. A worthy winner! You now have a choice to make. And that choice is between the very latest 3-litre family saloon car of your choice, or a luxury holiday for you, your wife and children, to . . . Honolulu! Which is it to be?'

'I'll take the holiday please,' said Henry straight away.

'Henry,' said the presenter, 'many people in the audience and at home would have chosen the 3-litre saloon car, yet you have chosen the holiday. Tell us about your choice.'

'Well, the wife and I haven't been able to afford a decent holiday for many years now. I don't earn so much, and we've a pretty large family.'

'How many children, Henry? If you don't mind me asking?'

'Sixteen children . . .' said Henry, clearing his throat.

The audience went wild.

The cameras stayed on Henry's smiling face for a full minute. The audience at home could not see the anxiety on other faces – those of the presenter, the producer, and other company officials in the wings.

Ten days later, after the celebrations were over, the letter arrived. It was from the TV company. It was short and to the point. Henry was disqualified. He had broken the rules, it said. There was to be no holiday for him and his family.

First impressions

Write the letter from the TV company to Henry. Unlike the one in the story, your letter should include the most likely reason for Henry's disqualification.

If you are in any doubt about the 'most likely' reason, even after re-reading the story, put down any reason that you may have come across in the text.

Discuss your answers

Read your letters to each other. Have you all come up with the same reason, or are there differences? Is there such a thing as 'the most likely reason'?

Investigating together

There are 4 possible reasons for Henry's disqualification (some of them rather far-fetched!). Search for them carefully.

Additional questions

1. What kind of game was 'Your Turn Now'? How do you suppose it was played?
2. Was there anything dishonest about Henry's statements? Any particular one?
3. How do you suppose he was found out?

Conclusions

Report back to the whole group.

Change of Mind

Does your Mum let you go shopping by yourself? Does she count the change when you get back? Mine does, every time! I suppose I don't blame her. She remembers a time I went for some fish and chips. Fish and chips for three, and it nearly cost £8! It was one day last summer . . .

My Mum had been to town with my younger sister. She had got back late.

'Karen!' she called out. 'I want you!'

'What do you want?' I asked.

'We're starving, Sharon and me. Be a love and get us some fish and chips. I haven't time to cook, and my feet are killing me. There's money in my purse.'

I went over to my Mum's bag. I looked through her purse.

'Is this all you've got?' I asked, holding up some brand-new £10 notes. 'Haven't you got any change?'

'Sorry, dear,' said my Mum, 'all my change went on bus fares. If that's all there is, you make sure you get the right change.'

I took the purse and crossed the room.

'You're not taking my purse, girl. Just one of those notes. Heavens above! There's £50 in there!'

I ran all the way to the shop. It wasn't far. Sometimes there were long queues, but not if you were there soon after twelve. When I got there, the queue wasn't so bad. Julie and Ann Davis were waiting just ahead of me. They are sisters. Julie is in my class at school. They'd just come back from their holiday in Spain. They were lovely and brown. And they had just collected their holiday snaps. There were hundreds of them – of the hotel; their Mum and Dad by the swimming pool; their Dad wearing a knotted handkerchief on his head; Julie and Ann wearing their bikinis.

'Who's this?' I asked. I had come to a snap of a dark fellow with a moustache. Julie blushed and snatched it.

'That's Manuel,' said Ann laughing. 'He was a waiter at the hotel. Julie fell madly in love with him.'

'Let's have a look, Julie. Go on!'

'Next, please! Hey, are you three wanting to be served?'
'Sorry,' I said, 'three cod and chips, please.'
Julie and Ann ordered theirs too. Then Julie showed me her
photo.

'Hey! He looks really dishy! Did he speak any English?'

'Three cod and chips and your change, love. Next?'

'Thanks,' I said.

'Did he?'

'Did he what?' asked Julie.

'Did he speak English?'

'Just a few words.'

'He taught her some Spanish,' said Ann. '*Gratias* means "thank you", and *te amore* means "I love you"!'

We carried on talking outside the shop for a few minutes. The fish and chips were getting cold, so I said goodbye and ran home.

'Where've you been?' my Mum shouted. 'We're starving!'

'Sorry, Mum,' I said. 'I met Julie. She was showing me her holiday photos. She's been to Spain.'

'Never mind that! Where's my change?' she demanded.

'Here,' I said and I laid it on the table.

'That's not right, girl! You haven't spent over £7, have you? There's only £2 odd here!'

'Oh, Lord!' I said, 'I was . . .'

'Get those chips down you. Then we're going right back to the shop.'

The shop owner was nice enough. He remembered serving me alright. But he didn't remember the £10 note. He went to his till and opened it. He showed us a huge bundle of £10 notes. Did we know which was ours? If we didn't, he was sorry. He couldn't help us.

'You can see my point,' he was saying.

My Mum was getting angry, so I stood back. There was going to be a row. Mum was going red in the face. Then I remembered something.

'Mum! Mum!' I called. 'I know how to sort this out! Calm down. I'm going back to the house for your purse. Wait while I get back!'

I was there and back in under five minutes. But I was gasping so much, the man couldn't have understood what I was trying to say. Anyway I opened my Mum's purse and was showing him the other £10 notes, and his face changed. He went to the till and got out his pile of £10 notes.

'Okay, okay,' he said after a second or two. 'My mistake. I'll get your proper change. Three cod and chips was £2.10. That means £7.90 change. Thank goodness that's sorted!' he said with a smile. We thanked him and left the shop.

My mum was puzzled. Why had I run back for her purse? I explained several times. In the end, I think she understood.

But neither of us ever understood the other thing. You see, we'd gone home and reckoned up all our money. And somehow we had ended up with more money than we'd started with!

First impressions

Write down the conversation that Karen had with her mother after they left the shop. Karen is trying to explain why she had run home for her Mum's purse. No more than half a page.

If you are having problems, re-read the story. An important clue comes up early on, before Karen sets off for the shop.

Discuss your answers

Read out your answers to each other.
Discuss any problems you may have had and any differences of opinion.
Establish which main clue comes early on in the story.

Investigating together

Try to sort out how Karen and her Mum had ended up with more money than they'd started with. Also, why there had been a mistake over the change in the first place.

Conclusions

Report back to the whole group.

The Ace of Diamonds

Lady Fitzwilliam would have to sell it. There was no other way. The family all agreed. Fitzwilliam Hall was in desperate need of repair. The windows were rotten; the chimneys on the west wing were leaning dangerously; the roof was letting in water in several places. She would have to sell the Fitzwilliam Diamond, or Fitzwilliam Hall would collapse.

The diamond had been 'in the family' for hundreds of years. Sir Henry de Fitzwilliam had fought with Sir Francis Drake against the Spanish Armada in 1588. Furthermore, he had been with Drake on his famous voyage round the world. It had been on this voyage that he had 'come by' the diamond after a sea skirmish somewhere off the Barbary Coast. On his return, the diamond had been taken to a master-jeweller. It had been set in a delicate gold ring, and given to his wife, the Lady Edwina.

It now sat in the strongest bank vault in the city of London. Sadly it was too valuable to be kept at Fitzwilliam Hall. In fact, Lady Fitzwilliam hardly ever saw it.

News of the sale of the ring was on the front page of every newspaper. The press were demanding interviews. She appeared on radio and TV several times. Here she was asked questions that fascinated the public.

Was she worried by the so-called 'jinx' on the ring? Hadn't some of her ancestors tried to sell the ring? And hadn't they come to a sticky end?

No, she said, she wasn't going to lose any sleep over this. She was more worried by a chimney falling through the roof.

Was she wearing the famous ring now?

No, she wasn't, she said. The Fitzwilliam Diamond was safely tucked up in a nice strong bank vault. The one she was wearing was an exact copy. She had had it made about 1930. She had worn this one ever since in the normal way. The original was only brought out on very special occasions, like Court occasions, Royal weddings and so on. Yes, at Prince Charles' wedding recently.

Could she tell the difference?

Well, she thought she could have done when she was a lot younger, but only with great difficulty. But nowadays she was an old lady and her eyesight was poor. She now relied on the experts, she said with a chuckle.

Was she going to the auction herself?

Of course she was! She wouldn't miss it for the world!

How much was she hoping it would fetch?

She didn't know that. She had been told that it might fetch as much as £2 million. She would be happy with this sum, she said. It would pay for all the repairs to Fitzwilliam Hall. She couldn't allow it to turn into a ruin. Not after more than five hundred years in her family. She just wanted to die with a clear conscience and all her affairs in order.

The day of the auction arrived. There were dealers from all over the world. Americans, Germans, Arabs – all packed into the small auction room. The tension was mounting. Outside, the sky was black and ominous. Thunderstorms were forecast. Huge security guards stood around nervously, waiting for proceedings to begin. And some of the tension may have reached the normally calm auctioneer. For when the diamond was, at last, brought in, he was visibly seen to stumble before reaching the platform. Only the timely help from a bystander in catching the diamond, saved it and the auctioneer from crashing to the ground.

As the diamond was finally put on view, there were loud gasps. This was surely the finest diamond in the world?

The auctioneer called for silence. The bidding started at £1 million. In no time it had reached one million eight hundred thousand pounds. It was at this point that proceedings were interrupted by a loud and high-pitched whistle from the middle of the room. As all eyes turned towards the source of the noise, Lady Fitzwilliam's voice could be heard. Her hearing-aid was on the blink, she was shouting to Barlow, her manservant. Would he hurry up and fix it?

But no sooner than the bidding had resumed, there was another interruption. A giant flash of lightning suddenly put out all the lights, and the auction room was plunged into darkness. But only for a couple of seconds, for almost immediately the emergency generators had been switched on, and everything brought back to normal. The auctioneer apologised, and the bidding resumed at a brisk pace.

It was a full five minutes after the hammer had finally fallen, that Lady Fitzwilliam's hearing-aid burst back into life. She was told that the diamond had been sold to an Arab prince for £5 million.

It was only by chance that Lady Fitzwilliam was watching the television news a year later. She hardly ever watched TV. But what was this?

'Sheikh Ahmed's London home was last night raided by jewel thieves. They took jewellery which is thought to be worth over £1 million. The thieves made off with most of the prince's valuable collection. The Fitzwilliam Diamond, however, was left in the safe. This famous diamond was recently sold to the Sheikh for £5 million. Police believe that the job was done by amateurs who were disturbed just in time. A police spokesman said: 'Expert thieves would have gone for the Fitzwilliam Diamond straight away''.'

'Well, well!' said Lady Fitzwilliam to herself. 'I suppose they know what they are talking about. I wonder . . .'

As she reached to turn off the television, a little smile spread across her face and she started to chuckle.

?

First impressions

Was the police spokesman right? *Had* the jewel thieves bungled? Lady Fitzwilliam is thinking there may be another explanation. Maybe more? Briefly

finish off what you think she may be thinking.
No more than half a page.

There are many possible endings, so you shouldn't
be stuck for something to write.

Discuss your answers

Read out your answers to each other.
You have probably come up with a variety of
answers. Are they all acceptable?

Investigating together

First, think about the incidents at the auction.
Discuss how these may be relevant to the later jewel
robbery, and in what way. Study the story.

Next, explore all the other reasons why the
Fitzwilliam Diamond may have been left in the safe.
There are 8 or more possibilities. Have fun!

Conclusions

Report back to the whole group.